YOUR KNOWLEDGE HAS VALUE

Shree Prasad Devkota

Centralized Education System leads to Underdevelopment and Social Conflict

GRIN Verlag

Bibliografische Information der Deutschen Nationalbibliothek:

Die Deutsche Bibliothek verzeichnet diese Publikation in der Deutschen National-
bibliografie; detaillierte bibliografische Daten sind im Internet über http://dnb.d-
nb.de/ abrufbar.

Imprint:

Copyright © 2014 GRIN Verlag GmbH
Druck und Bindung: Books on Demand GmbH, Norderstedt Germany
ISBN: 978-3-656-82596-8

This book at GRIN:

http://www.grin.com/en/e-book/282653/centralized-education-system-leads-to-
underdevelopment-and-social-conflict

GRIN - Your knowledge has value

Der GRIN Verlag publiziert seit 1998 wissenschaftliche Arbeiten von Studenten, Hochschullehrern und anderen Akademikern als eBook und gedrucktes Buch. Die Verlagswebsite www.grin.com ist die ideale Plattform zur Veröffentlichung von Hausarbeiten, Abschlussarbeiten, wissenschaftlichen Aufsätzen, Dissertationen und Fachbüchern.

Visit us on the internet:

http://www.grin.com/

http://www.facebook.com/grincom

http://www.twitter.com/grin_com

CENTRALIZED EDUCATION SYSTEM LEADS UNDERDEVELOPMENT AND
SOCIAL CONFLICT

Abstract

Barrier to the inclusive education in school leads unrest and underdevelopment in the society. The paper focused on the ongoing process of education system in Nepal after the advent of democracy in 1951AD, to till the Peoples Movement of 2004 AD. Six decades political unrest brought drastic change in the socio-economic and education in Nepal. Though, it was unknown, people followed social pattern in the education system. SSRP was implemented with inclusive education along with the policy of mother tongue approach; led fully fledged democratic norms and the principles in education policy in Nepal. Now the time has come, planners, educators, researcher felt the need of inclusive education in the context of Nepal to promote and preserve cultural diversity.

Table of Content

Background

Education is the strongest weapon to change the whole world (Nelson Mandela). Of course yes whole set of development starts from the base of education. Society we live today is heterogeneous in nature. It is the post modern era, having the ideology of rethinking of thinking; defamiliarity of familiarity, deconstruction of construction in every field of development. In this context the present day education is overemphasized in technique rather than the feeling of oneness. Nevertheless, technical education is necessary for physical development too. Education begins with value judgment and belief in reality of life. It begins in the hands of educator, who must understand oneself, and come up against established pattern. It is way to postmodernism era in education which gives diverse education to all with value judgment in each individual's life. It is the era of openness and the way to expose individual talent through education process. I am in great dilemma regarding the kind of education prevailing in our country. The policies are better but, implementation part is very weak, it is due to lack of monitoring process. The right kind of education cultivates true relationship between not only individual but, also between the individual and the society; above all, help the individual to understand oneself and their responsibility in the society (Krishnamurti, 2009, p. 34). Culturally diverse society needs inclusive education to overcome social problem. Nepal is in need of inclusive education in a sense that those children who are disabled in one way or other has right to get according to their capability. Still today, it is clear that large numbers of children who struggle daily with additional hardships are not getting the chance to improve their lives through education. This means, of course, they are caught in a spiral of low expectation, low esteem and low income (UNICEF, 2003). Who are normal children to get education? Nevertheless, all of us are not able to perform every things at a time that's why we are also disabling in one way other. Of course yes, brailed which are useful for the visually impaired children are not for the normal children. In these sense normal children seems abnormal for disabled. It's very serious matter for those who work in this field. In next paragraph I have pointed out the inclusive education policy Government of Nepal from the critical perspective.

Inclusive Education Policy in Nepal

The reconstructions theory advocates that the school should take the lead to change the society. Schools have more responsibility to transmit knowledge; they have the mission to transform society as well. The theorist think critically and with full of skill in this system, students learn to handle controversy and recognize multiple perspective. It is hard to implement inclusive education which construct the knowledge of diversity in schools

The end of Rana regime in 1951 AD is the beginning of new era in the history of Nepal. The democratic system prevailed with much more enthusiasm and paved the way in the field of building infrastructure. The then Government adopted some policies in favor of educating people. Nepal National Education Planning Commission, (1954), was set up as the historic achievement as it was the first ever foreign influence Wood Commission in Nepal. It gave system. Nonetheless, the policy acknowledged the role of education for social transformation and decentralization. But, this policy was unable to recognize to grab the spirit of political change, as well as failed to recognize the multilingual education and education for the disabled; instead it imposed linguistic restriction which discouraged the spirit of multilingualism. It was unable to recognize children's management and teaching. The conservative policy made the extinction of number of language from our country. Later on All Round National Education Commission, (1962), was set up and during sixties expansion of private school system was introduced with English language teaching. It was suggested for implementing free and compulsory primary education. However, the policy failed to support neither the diversified education system nor the policy of special education to the special children. It was in 1971-75, New Education System Plan was implemented, and the school came directly under the management and ownership of Government. It means the centralized system was adopted with the restructuring primary school from 1-3 grades. The text books were developed but, not according to the cultural setting of a nation. However, emphasized was given to use Nepali language in school. It is said that Nepali became a part of the nationalistic movement across the country. Similarly National Education Commission, (1990), the policy focused on non- Nepali language in the school. The priority was given to those children with multilingual rather than the integrated system of education. Similarly National Education Commission, (1990), was introduced with the policy focused on non-Nepali language in the school. The priority was given to those children from multilingual committees to learn their local languages. The Government has focused on diverse languages but, not the priority for disabled children. By, 2004, vulnerable community development plan was introduced the social inclusion and integrating disadvantaged children in primary school. The plan also emphasized the need for targeted interventions for girls, children from dalit, indigenous and ethnic minorities in the school. Society having diverse ethnic communities like that of Nepal must come forward for bridging social relations with democratic governance and acceptance of the ethnic groups to be part of the social fabric are relevant to manage conflict through inclusive education. When the diversity is treated as the neglected dimension, there is deprivation of the specific communities which finally create injustice in the society. This is the serious matter in the context of Nepal and deprived communities may not have the feeling of nationality, which threaten the nation. Furthermore, we need to analyze the policy adopted in the Interim Constitution of Nepal 2007, it has declared education as the right of a citizens and primary education in the mother tongue was emphasized with the idea of three language policy, they are- mother tongue, Nepali and English. To meet the learning activities School Sector Reform Plan (2009-2015), prioritized on meeting diverse learning needs of children of different social and cultural settings. It has found that the concept of 'entitlement' to support the education of marginalized communities the provision for 'minimum enabling condition' for every school. The ground reality in education system is totally different, still there is need to do lot in this field to bring inclusiveness in multiculturalism. When we talk about the education, there we find two types of education for children; they are special education and integrated education. The special education was started I1964 AD in Nepal at the school situated at Chet Bhawan Lajimpat for the visually impaired children. After the world conference at Salamasscer in Spain in 1994 AD, the new concept of inclusion education started in the different part of the world. The inclusion education is the process of addressing and responding to the diversity of the need of all learners in the classroom in the school and in the society and here by reducing exclusion within and from education no matter what causes the exclusion could be (Inspired by UNESCO 2000).

Today the diversity cultural education is referred as the inclusion education; it does not mean the special education only. During the BPEP 2nd phase special education project (1993-1999), was to establish resource classes with residential facilities for children and different disabilities. It is obvious that the children with disabilities were segregate from main society and from families. The special education section had to change, not the vision, but strategies for the special education programme (Holst 2001). There are several international discussion for nearly eleven years among the INGO, NGO regarding the interest of disability issues. The UN Rules on the Equalization of Opportunities for Person with Disabilities was adopted by all the UN member states in 1993. The concept of definition was suggested regarding disability. The genuine clarification has been given in term of disability, which should not be understood as a defect of individual but as a relation between a person and the environment that restrain equal opportunities. It is true to say that in certain situation a person can be disabled while in other situation the same person is not disabled at all (UN 1994). In the same manner the Dakar Declaration of 2000 AD gave the concept of Education for All (EFA). It is further more steps towards the inclusion education pattern.

Education is in inclusive in nature if it is able to accept holistic approach of functional structuralism. The theory like Information Processing is relevant in this context. Disabled children in the school learn through their sharp mind. The mind makes meaning through symbol processing structure of fixed body of knowledge. It describes how information is gathered, proceed received, stored and retrieved from the mind. As far concern the education to disabled have become challenges to the Government of Nepal. The Government of Nepal has ratified the Convention of the Rights of the Child (1989), and is a signatory of the declaration Education for All (1990) and the Salamanca Declaration (1994). These documents call for the provision of public education to all children, regardless of their physical, intellectual, emotional, social, linguistic, or other conditions. The Department of Education had taken up the challenge of initiating inclusive education in Nepal. Governmental agencies such as the National Planning Commission Secretariat, the Ministry of Women, Children and Social Welfare, the Ministry of Education, the Ministry of Health, the Ministry of Finance, the Ministry of Local Development and the Social Welfare Council are working for disability in various ways. Several initiatives to provide integrated and inclusive education for children with disabilities have also been taken by charity organizations, religious institutions, local NGOs and international organizations. The vision for better world only comes through diversity education system. There are certainly too many problems while implementing world concept in the local level. We have not studied deeply to introduce inclusive education system. I have been teaching in the school level since last eighteen years though it is difficult to find out the root cause of snail's pace in the education policy of the Government. There is misconception among the teaching staff about the inclusiveness. The idea is about the ethnicity only, it is not the reality, and physically disabled are also the part of school education. The curriculum must be suitable for multiple disable and for the normal children. For that we have to go shortly through the situation analyses of disabled children. If they are excluded from the school we have to face more and more problems in society.

Situation Analysis of the Disabled Children

According to the progressivism theorist suggest that that education should be of integration of thinking, feeling and doing. It is said that learners must be active enough to solve the various problems through their experiences. It was in the year 1971; a numerous studies have been conducted by the Government institutions NGOs and INGOs for the estimation of disabled people in Nepal. It was in 1971, census the estimated 1.5 percent of the population over 10 years had disabilities. Later on in the disability sample survey of 1980, reported a prevalence rate of disability of three percent of the population. The very next year in1981 census estimated the five percent of population had disability. According to the survey, mental retardation in Nepal in 1989, estimated 4.9 percent of the population had mental retardation. In this condition what is the condition of people who are facing such a disability in learning process. Not only that there is prevalence of deafness and ear diseases, more than 16 percent and visual impairment. A five-district Disabled Situation Analysis of Nepal conducted by APROSC in 1998 estimated that 3.4 per cent of the population in the study area had disabilities. The Situation Analysis of Disability in Nepal (NPC/UNICEF/New Era, 2001) estimates the national prevalence of disability at 1.63 per cent of the population. In this study, a person is considered disabled if he/she cannot perform the daily activities of life considered normal for a human being within the specified age group and where the person needs special care, support and some kind of rehabilitation service. In this situation crystal clear planning is necessary to implement inclusive education.

Inclusive Education Practices

There has been certain approach in the school education including disable children in the same room which is regarded as the inclusive education. To do away, not to remain close to each other or not to accept others theory is said to be deviance in a society (Subedi, 2010). If I have become the best example in the existing society it is sure there more chances

of ruining from those people who had flatter. It is psychic phenomenon of an individual. In
the long acculturation process take place. Diffusion refers to fusion of all the cultural group
surviving together for individual aims rather than the national interest. The name and fame at
the end of selfish journey give rise to popularity in the nation and rest of the world too.
Though, it is not the concept of inclusion but, it is way to inclusiveness in the social setting.
Of course yes there is power hegemony and antagonistic nature among the few; others are in
the sake of living for a day. Now I draw the turning point in the education for all (EFA), is it
accessible to all from Himalayan region to terai region? No not at all, government at the
central level meeting in capital city is not a solution of inclusive education. I attended the
seminar on the topic regarding 'exceptional children', in 2001 on the month of January. The
delegates of South Korea and representatives from various parts of the world discuss the
matter of special children and their education system. The very year UN Secretary General
Kofi Annan said, *"Our biggest challenge in this new century is to take an idea that seems
abstract -sustainable development -- and turn it into a reality for the entire world's
people."UNSG 2001.* I being the student of anthropology puzzled just hearing their debates
of their own thinking and of their countries ideology. After ten year of loin 2013 when I
joined as the student of Kathmandu University M. Phil. in education (Development Studies),
come to the point their concept of inclusive education system was for disabled children in
some particular areas only. Later days I didn't attend. Today the system of education to the
school children is changing slowly but rapidly in accordance with world scenario. The
concept of pre schooling and Maria Montessori based education has started in the private
boarding schools. It is giving quality education or not , it is another part of judgment,
nevertheless after 1992 the moss rooming of private boarding is the demand of government to
educate Nepali children through English medium. The credit of better results in SLC from
these private schools gives government the great pride having successful education. , though
they take the credit of success. Every subject are taught, there is extracurricular activities and
in many school disabled children are getting the education, specially visually impaired
children and hearing impaired children are getting the better education facilities. I come to
know after attaining the seminar and field visit during my study period. Till 2001 there were
47 resource centers for visually impaired children now the number have increased to more
than 50 in the different districts of Nepal. The most common type of disability in Nepal is
multiple disabilities; it accounts for 31 per cent of disabled people. Among those with
multiple disabilities, 48 per cent have hearing and speech disability. Loco-motor disability
accounts for 28 per cent of people with disabilities. Mental retardation and epilepsy account

for 13 per cent (NPC/UNICEF/New Era, 2001). In such a critical situation government has to work in accordance with the suggestion given by the educationists. That is why there is special education council for the special students. Till today if we look into the progress report we find only visually impaired students had appeared SLC examination and have joined higher studies. I personally asked the central committee president of NAB and found that one or two students from few schools appeared SLC examination. There is inclusive policy as stated by Mr. Madav Aryal whom I met during my study period. He had played the active role to enroll disabled students in the schools of town area searching from the remote village. Being the country representative he explained to say the irony that parents hide their disable children thinking that it is the previous life curse. They remain dirty for a month too, it is really pitiful situation. Nevertheless, the time has changed their voice is listened in the Parliament too. There is Right to get education, food, proper care by the parents or any social organization to these abnormal children. It is obviously known that we cannot change the society within a night; takes long time see the society as we have thought. Too many internal organization along with the local organization are helping disabled children giving them education and vocational training. NAB, NAWB and Khagendra Nawajiwan Sangha, Nepal Netra Jyoti Sangha are giving everything to disabled children and people too. To my perception it is the way to inclusive education.

Inclusiveness is Multiculturalism

Many of the educators had pointed out the importance of multiculturalism. According to Woolfolk (2002), multiculturalism is one response to the increasing diversity of school population as well as to fulfill the equality of all the groups. The main objective is to prepare students for diverse cultural society. That is why teachers must develop positive self concept among the children of disability. We have to bear in mind that there is always influence of one culture to another in the society; it is acculturization process. This is how the society functions, in the multiculturalism environment in the class.

The revolution of 2004 AD brought the drastic change in the country. Nepal is a secular nation with the identity of cultural pluralism. At first it has the direct effect on the education. Nepal is the land of ethnic diversity with multi cultural practices. Hence, multiculturalism is the process where every individual and group could express their ideas. The same method is applicable in education system which has become no more foreign issue, it is totally the pure issue of Nepal and curriculum must be inclusive in nature. Therefore, we are able to survive in the society; otherwise there is chances of the extinct of any minor cultural groups who speak local dialects among their own small community. For example Kusunda people are almost extinct from Nepal. Inclusiveness is only the way for the survival of all these dialects. On the other hand it may be threat to the nation, if it is not preserved in time. As a whole what is necessary is the proper educational planning. Expert educationists and intellectual personalities must think of a cultural pluralism issue. The plan for giving basic education to children in mother tongue (local dialects) is the best way of inclusiveness pattern. But, in the context of Nepal, though the priority has been given for the local level dialects, students who attend the school are from different castes, religion, ethnicity etc. The heterogeneous classroom teaching practices prevail which is common throughout the country. Within this heterogeneity there is the question of dalits, madeshies and other marginalized, and victim children who need education in school in better environment. To clarity the topic I have pointed out the incident, as a researcher in the Government school I overcome with peculiar incident of discriminating people to people. Dalit students were not allowed to sit with high caste Bramin and Chhetri students, not only that no mongol children were accepted to sit with neither them during lunch time nor they were allowed to in social feast if they were permitted had to take this feast at last. I come to know the activities of Bramin teachers who think themselves as superior than others. I strongly opposed them but, my aim went in vain. It was the Dy-function in the society. It was great challenge for the dalits to get their rights. Today the policy has changed even the high castes students know the reality and the consequences of social discrimination. Frankly speaking, high castes people are not safe. So, they are forced to adopt the policy of equality and inter cultural relationship. School has become the best place to unite the people in the community. It is the duty of teacher to understand the issue and problem of diverse society (Subedi, 2010). I agree with the decade of 1960; emancipation through the notion of multicultural emergence in the west (Gross, 2010).

The education for all (EFA), is the slogan only; still main focus is on primary education only. Though it is post modern era, the modernization started in Nepal after the advent of democracy in Nepal in 1951AD, with concept of educating people. The policy in document is far better than its implication practically. That is why Nepal has faced the major challenge in promoting a more inclusive system in education. There was society with diverse cultural practices, but, unknowingly people practiced inclusion in the past, today the same issue has emerged through the government level to the bottom level. Actually, inclusive education is a border term which covers the wide range of area in every governmental sectors one of them is education sector which is the backbone of the nation. Inclusive education means responding to the diversity (Basnet & Dr. Baskota, 2010) which plays the vital role in recognizing culture. I don't think so, that the education is inclusive unless it carries the voice of all the people. Right kind of education in the right place according to the demand is the inclusive education system.

Challenges of Inclusive Education

Nepal being the economically poor country has to face numerous problems which are unable to solve within a short period of time. It needs deep thinking and proper planning with educationists, researchers and governmental body who are real responsible for the betterment of the school inclusive education system. The multicultural process and the part of pluralism although same, the priority must be given to school education system with inclusive character. Some of the points on the challenges issues are given below:-

I.   Though it is the post modern era there is still the lack of the concept of educators who think of proper planning in the field of inclusive system.

II.   Society is heterogeneous in nature it is difficult to teach students in their own mother tongue. Nevertheless, the concept of learning local dialects is in rise. However, there may be misconception for those Nepali speaking community.

III. Giving priority to disabled children is beyond the capacity of the government of Nepal, due to extreme topographical features.

IV.   The concept of post positivism in comprehensive inclusion of diverse education policy is today's need. But, still follows the education of pre modern era.

V.   There is need of thinking beyond the school boundary for those who do not go to school. Non formal school needs to run with full fledge resources.

VI.   Due to the unstable government administrative system and the lack of planner in the education in mainstream schools.

VIII Most special education programmes are donor-funded. Donors have a great influence   over   programme design.

IX   There are few examples of good practice models for inclusive education. They are relatively new, and need to be strengthened to make programmes more child- and disability-friendly.

Conclusion

The study of the situation of disabled children and inclusion education in the school level is the key to today's study. Very soon government is launching its programme declaring basic primary education from class one to eight and secondary level from class nine to twelve with inclusive ideology.

I.   We need to prepare the curriculum according to diverse cultural practices..

II. Government has to survey disabled children in a micro level otherwise it is very difficult to find out the exact number of disable children.

III. Multicultural policy has to be adopted to give equal priority to dalits, madishes, and native and marginalized people in mainstream.

IV. All the national and international organization which are working for the betterments of disabled children, needs progress in their life style.

V.   In Nepal, the division between special and general education policy clouds the development of an inclusion policy. The government's education policy categorizes three types of education, namely, education for children in general, education for children with disabilities (mainly in the form of special education and integrated education.(NPC/UNICEF2001).

VI. If the government remains unstable due to political unrest , the country finds difficulty in progress in education. It has to be the voice of every disable children in the Parliament.

Recommendations

I.   Till now the disabled people are regarded as the second class citizen that is why people with disability have a right to take part in the state affairs as the equal citizen.

II. Instead of giving special education to the disabled children they are to be included to mainstream schools. This attitude creates normal children to accept the world of diversity.

III. The policy of priority and legislative provisions must ensure children with disabilities access to schools.

However, policy formulation and implementation cannot not be effective unless the government gives attention to the quality of education, physical infrastructure, teacher training, support staff in the classroom and, most importantly, to the misconceptions and

attitudinal barriers hindering the acceptance of inclusive education (UNICEF2001).
Otherwise there shall be unrest in the society which ultimately leads to underdevelopment in
the nation. Focusing the inclusive policy in the present context is way to federalism.

References

Anon (2001*), When will 'education for all' include children with disabilities?* International *Rehabilitation Review, 51(1).*

Basnet, S. & Dr. Baskota, (2010), *Inclusive education for transhumance group in Himalayas: Education policy challenges for Nepal. Journal of* Kathmandu University. Publisher

ESP,(2011), Alliance for Social Dialogue, Education Strategic Plan, Battisputali, Kathmandu..Publisher.

Govt. of Nepal,(2066-72), School Area Implementation Planning. *Education of Ministry. Author.*

Gross, S (2010), Inequality and emancipation: An educational approach. Journal of Kathmandu University. Publisher.

Holst, J. (2000), *The challenge of special need education, Seminar paper, presented a*t Dhulikhel.

Holst, J. (2001), *Special education in Nepal current challenges, seminar paper, presented at* Kritipur Tribhuvan University Hall.

UNICEF/New Era (2001). A situation analysis of disability in Nepal. National Planning Commission, UNICEF and Nepal,

Ministry of Education (2010). *Program implementation guideline FY 2010/11.* Kathamndu. Author.

National Education Commission (1992). *A report of the national education Commission.* Kathamndu. Author.

Subedi, D. (2010), *Multicultural classroom issues in the Nepalese context. Journal of* Kathmandu University. Publisher